under the

influence

jacquelyn lee

under the influence

ISBN: 978-1984141620

Printed in the United States of America.

Written, edited, designed and self-published by Jacquelyn Lee.

Also by Jacquelyn Lee

mind over mother

to every child
who had to grow up
under the influence
this is for you

you should be proud of yourself
you have made it here safely
you have survived

you took what
you went through
by the throat
you deprived it
of its oxygen

you threw it to the ground
like a cigarette butt
you put out its flame
and you made it here

let this be your safe haven
let these words
help you understand
that your parent's mistakes
are not yours
let my story inspire you
to tell yours

but tread easy because
this is not a daydream
what you're about to read is
my worst nightmare
– this is my story

would you ever write a book about your life
she asked
maybe
i replied

to those who encouraged me to
tell my story
you know who you are

trigger warning...

this book contains
highly sensitive content
related to...

abuse
abandonment
alcoholism
anxiety
bereavement
childhood trauma
death
depression
domestic violence
drug addiction
eating disorders
family dysfunction
grief
mental illness
self-harm
sexual abuse
suicide

& more

please don't forget to practice self-love
while reading and always

xoxo

preface...

...what if i had died instead of you?
...what if the body they found
hanging in the basement
was mine instead of yours?
...would they have said my death was all your fault,
the way they said your death was all mine?
...would they have told you
not to show up to my funeral,
the way they told me
not to show up to yours?
...would they have acted like they were my best friend
the way they acted like they were yours?
...would they have printed
my picture on tee shirts
and praised me,
even though they hated me?
...would they have wished
death upon you,
the way they continue to wish
death upon me?
...would they have threatened you,
the way they've threatened me?
...would they have given you
the hell they've given me?
oh, i wish i knew
what they would do
if i had died instead of you

rest in paradise, dad
here lies the pain, trauma & grief
you left behind

contents

chapter one
addiction...

Jack Daniel's was like a sixth member of our family
I don't have a single memory of my father
Without a bottle of it in his hand

Growing up with an alcoholic father
and Growing up without a father
are a pair of siamese twins conjoined at the hip
they may have minds of their own
but they are two of a kind, they are one and the same

Empty bottles of Jack Daniel's lined
the basement floor of a place we once called home

Our father took pride
in the amount of empty bottles on that basement floor
as if they were trophies

In actuality, those empty bottles
were filled with his deepest sorrow

Eventually,
Jack and Coke robbed all of Dad's money
his addiction led to the first eviction

We had 48 hours to pack up
our pride, our dignity, our shame

We moved from house to house across the same town
for four years, straight

Packing boxes became a normal routine
and stability became impossible to reach

Until one day, the instability slapped me in the face
and the cops came

I told them to get me away
from my father

And after that day
I never spoke to him, again

"Why do you move so often?"

~~Because my father is an addict.~~

~~Because our rent doesn't get paid.~~

~~Because every aspect of my life is unstable.~~

"Oh, I don't know."

Dad –

I forgive you for stealing my credit card to go to the liquor store.

I forgive you for giving me a stolen car (that was stolen back) for my high school graduation.

I forgive you for *borrowing* my $900 tax refund, and never paying me back.

I forgive you for telling me I was going to be nothing in life because I took a semester off from college.

I forgive you for making me pay for your cell phone bill when the roles should have been reversed.

I forgive you for making me spend my 18th birthday in a hotel room (and for making me pay $400 for it, myself) because our electricity got shut off.

I forgive you for leaving me no choice but to raise myself and my three younger siblings.

I forgive you for smashing the passenger-side window of the car with your bare hands while I was driving (and for making me lie and say someone broke into the car.)

I forgive you for the time I told you I was going to move out, so you went into my room and smashed everything.

And lastly, I forgive you for hitting me after eighteen years of telling me that *you'd kill* the first man to put his hands on me.

- *Ironically, you did.*

The thing about having
an alcoholic parent
is that no matter how many times
they've disappointed you,
you still believe them when
they tell you
things are going to get better

Even though you know
you're going to get crumbs,
you expect the whole cake
e v e r y
s i n g l e
t i m e

And so, I cleaned up
my father's mess
literally and figuratively
from the broken glass
on the living room floor
to the broken pieces
of my sibling's hearts

wow, you and your siblings are such great kids
thanks, we raised ourselves

grab a pen and paper

take the pain

they've caused you and

write,

write,

write,

until your fingers

bleed the pain

straight out of your heart

I am ~~strong~~
because you were ~~abusive~~

I am ~~a perfectionist~~
because you were ~~too hard on me~~

I am ~~a girl who has trust issues~~
because you were ~~a pathological liar~~

I am ~~a better person~~
because you were ~~an example of everything I don't want to be~~

I am ~~beyond my years~~
because you were ~~behind in yours~~

I am ~~disgusted by alcohol~~
because you were ~~addicted to it~~

Family dysfunction is
often concealed by broken smiles
the same way family photos often
cover up punched holes in walls

Blood is thicker than Water they say
then why has Water had to cleanse me of
the mess my Blood has made?

\-   *It's all a lie*

just because your home is physically safe
does not always mean it is mentally safe

a list of things that qualify as child abuse:

- swearing at your kids on a regular basis
- stealing money from your kids
- keeping your kids away from loved ones out of spite
- holding your kids back from chasing their dreams
- telling your kids they are a mistake
- telling your kids they are too fat or too skinny
- telling your kids they aren't smart enough because they were graded 90% on a test instead of 100%
- lying to your kids to manipulate them
- choosing drugs and alcohol over putting food in your kid's mouths
- making your kids fend for themselves

-   *you don't have to beat your kids for it to be abuse*

my sister's journal sat on her bedside table
in our bedroom that morning
staring at me with weary eyes,
it screamed *open me open me*

i listened to its screams
i opened it
only to find journal entries titled,
depression
anxiety
cutting

a split second later
my father called me
downstairs
the school just called
he said
they found out she's been cutting herself

- *coincidence or fate?*

My little sister
shouldn't have
had to cut her wrist
to deal with
the emotional pain
that our parents caused

My little brothers
shouldn't have
to live with
the anger issues
that our parents caused

Coming from a broken home
is so much more than
simply coming from a broken home

A broken home houses all of the
broken promises
broken hearts
broken relationships
and broken children
that are subject
to all of their parent's mistakes

Please believe me when I say
it is not your fault
that your parents couldn't fix
what was already b r o k e n

Please believe me when I say
that their mistakes are not and will never be
your fault

Their mistakes may be enough
to fill a thousand oceans

Their mistakes may be enough
to outnumber the stars in the night sky

But you are not
and will never be *one of them*

For you are not deserving of being called a star
you are the moon
you carry a light so bright, you control the ocean's tides

-   *to all of the kids that come from broken homes*

High out of his mind, he woke the entire house that night
it was the middle of August but he was
dressed in all black, in a winter coat and a ski mask

With a knife in his Hand and a crazed look in his Eyes
he hurried outside and he got into his van
leaving us to wonder where he was off to

We laughed it off, really, the dysfunction was customary
Until we woke up the next morning
to a phone call that he was behind bars
while his ex-girlfriend was in the emergency room
wearing his Hands around her neck
and his fists in her Eyes

I'm still not sure which charge was worse,
the domestic violence or the possession of cocaine?
either way, we didn't have to worry
after nearly dying, his ex-girlfriend dropped the charges
she thought she was saving us
but all she did was put us back in harm's way

Maybe if he would've went to prison
He would've learned that Cocaine
is not an excuse for beating women

Three years later, the same woman who walked around with
his Hands around her neck and his fists in her Eyes
did not believe me when I said
those same hands made my face go numb

Three years later, the same people who called my father
a woman-beating coke-head for battering his ex-girlfriend
did not believe that he could've possibly
laid a hand on his own daughter

but
where
is
your
mom?

- *a question I never wanted to answer*

my mother
quit her job
one day

                                          so, grandma
                                          told her
                                          that she was done
                                          enabling her

she told mom to
start working again
or else she'd have no choice
but to push her out of the nest

                                          but mom said
                                          that she didn't have to
                                          work and that God would
                                          provide for us

then grandma
told mom that
she needed to go
to the ~~mental~~ hospital
but mom refused

                                          so, months later
                                          we moved into
                                          a new house with our father
                                          and his girlfriend

at that time
we had no idea
that he would
become what
he soon became

Mom –

You can't just show up on Christmas and birthdays
if you aren't here the rest of the 365 days

- *we want your presence, not your presents*

Dysfunction is a vicious cycle
of abuse and neglect

As I
get older
I understand
why my
father
drank
himself
to his
deathbed

And why
my mother
chooses to
live a life
of delusion
and
neglects her
own children

But there is no excuse
we all have the power
to break the cycle

You simply
have to choose
to be better
than the cards
you were dealt

food
became
my
biggest
enemy
&
my
eating
disorder
became
my
best
friend
in
high
school

you grow up in a
family of women
who call themselves fat
when they're a size 2
and call themselves ugly
when they're the
most beautiful

and then they wonder why
their daughters leave their
dinner plates half-full
and start wearing make-up
in middle school

-    *vanity*

why are you doing this to me
my body said to me

as i was hurled over the
toilet with
a finger down my throat

please stop
my body cried
stop telling me that
i'm anything less
than perfect the way
i am

-     *to my body: you are perfect the way God created you*

while her father
was addicted to
doing lines

she was
addicted to
the lines on
her thighs

you're sixteen when
your father's best friend
starts making passes at you
if only you were eighteen
he'd say
i'd put a ring on your finger

this leads to him
following you
into your room after
you get out of the
shower and
grabbing your thigh
in the car after he picks
you up from work

it isn't much longer
until your dad
finds out,
chases him
around the house
with a knife,
and goes
outside to
slash the tires
on his car

after that he
pulls the hair
out of your head
and says
thanks for ruining my friendship

    -   *it took me three years to realize it was never my fault*

we had a beautifully trimmed
twelve foot Christmas tree
in our living room

it stood tall and proud
for everyone to see

but this beautiful tree
had no presents
underneath it
on Christmas Day

just as
our father always had
his best face on
for the world to see

but behind closed doors,
gave us nothing

my father
dated women
who used him
for his money
and then he'd
wonder why
his kids were
going hungry

you must love yourself
more than you love those
who hurt you

Abuse has no
sense of time
Trust me, it does not matter
if you were abused
for a lifetime or a season of time
There is no difference
The trauma is all the same
Do not ever let anyone
tell you otherwise

The first few years of not being abused
does not make up for
the last few years of constant abuse
Trust me, the good times
do not ever cancel out the bad

my father
used to drink
coffee with
milk and sugar
in the morning

but eventually
he replaced that
milk and sugar

with jack and coke
instead

-   *addiction*

my brother was thirteen the first time he had to
tie himself to our father
to stop him from going into the basement
and tying that same rope
around his neck

it happened so often
we had a name for it
suicide watch

alcohol-induced suicidal thoughts
and texts to the family group-chat that read
i just can't do this anymore,
please take care of each other
i love you, babies
don't come into the garage tonight

followed by piercing screams and painful sobs
dad, please don't do this
we'd cry

and after we escaped the hell that we called home
we were told that it was our fault that our father
killed himself

but, would it have
been *our fault*
if he would have
done it then?

how do they
not understand
that his mind
was trying to
destroy itself
for years?

they wanted me to
hide everything i went through
in the back of my closet
and let it turn to dust

they wanted me to
burn everything i went through
to the ground,
take the ashes and
paint a beautiful picture
out of them

they wanted me to
take that beautiful picture
and hang it up
in every museum
for the whole world to see

they wanted me to
keep the darkness
hidden in the shadows
of the wilderness

but instead i
took that darkness
out of the wilderness
and brought it into the light

i gave it to the sun
i asked her to
shine it in their eyes
i asked her to
burn them with the truth

they wanted me to
conceal the truth
about my life

the way i conceal the
bags underneath my eyes

what they fail to realize is
the bags underneath my eyes
carry the abuse, the pain, the trauma
that i've been through in my life

i refuse to conceal them anymore

my father called me in his room that night
drunk, high, out of his mind
with a face full of tears he said
i never told anyone this but
my sister used to molest me
when i was younger
she used to use me as her sex toy
that's why i'm so messed up

in that moment,
i wasn't sure if i believed him

but after everything
it all makes sense now

-   *drunk words // sober thoughts*

stop blaming yourself
for your parent's mistakes
stop feeling guilty for
what they've put you through
sometimes toxic parents
have to be broken up with too

chapter two
withdrawal...

June 11th, 2017 –

After my cousin's sweet sixteen, my dad came home a drunken mess. He swore that I left the party with my three younger siblings *without telling him.* Yet, we told him that we were leaving – three separate times. It was ten o'clock on a Sunday night. My younger siblings had school in the morning, and I was exhausted. All we wanted to do was go home and go to bed.

On top of that – my cell phone died, so I didn't know that my father called me seventeen times while I was driving home. He got home shortly after we did. He angrily opened the front door. And ironically – at the same exact time, I stepped out of my bedroom. He shouted out to my younger siblings and me, *"Get downstairs!"* And he demanded that we all sit down on the couch. He yelled at us for leaving the party *without telling him.*

Drunk and disorderly – he picked up a wooden stool and threw it across the living room. Before my brain could even process what was going on, the wooden stool hit into a glass shelf. The glass came shattering down, just as our life as we knew it did that night. I screamed in fear. In-between my screams I muttered, *"Wh-who even are you anymore? You aren't the father I once knew."*

After that, something I never thought would happen, happened. All that I'm going to say is, I lived eighteen years being able to say that my father has never put his hands on me.

My face was numb. My entire body was numb. The emotional pain my father caused me my entire life had now become physical. Tears ran down my cheeks as quickly as my brother jumped up and screamed, *"Why would you hit Jackie?!"* He got my father away from me, and I ran upstairs.

I had to make the biggest decision of my life. Do I stay in this life of dysfunction, or do I not? Do I continue to make excuses for my alcoholic father, or do I not? I was nervous. I was afraid. I was uneasy. All we wanted to do that night was go home and go to sleep. Yet, my father was downstairs, in a fist fight with my fifteen-year-old brother after I'd just gotten back-handed across the face by him – for absolutely no reason.

My younger sister and I sat on her bed together – crying in fear and distress. My first instinct told me to text my aunt and my grandma about what just happened. My aunt called me right away. I spoke to her and my uncle about calling the police. Looking back, I had no idea that they'd soon become our legal guardians. My father began banging on our bedroom door, threatening to bust it down if we didn't open it. I instantly hung up, hiding my phone under my sister's comforter. We let him into our bedroom, and he yelled at us repeatedly – for absolutely no reason.

We could smell the alcohol on his breath. My sister asked him, *"Why did you hit Jackie?"* And my father replied, *"I'll hit you, too."* I knew then – we just couldn't stay in that house any longer. After what felt like forever, my father walked out of the room. He proceeded to go downstairs and began fighting with his twenty-four-year-old girlfriend. From the yelling that I heard, they both had knives in their hands. It really sounded like they were going to kill each other.

I called my aunt back – and I decided that it was best if she called the cops for me. So then, we waited. When the cops arrived, my dad was passed out drunk in his bed. From there – all I can say is, I never spoke another word to my father – and I will never have the chance to do so again.

"But, he only hit you once."
"But, you don't even have any bruises."
"But, he's your father.
He was just disciplining you."
"You know he still loves you, though.
He didn't mean it."

-   *what shallow people say to domestic violence victims*

but he only hit you once
they ignorantly said

what they fail to realize
is that once is enough

\-   *if he hits you once, he'll hit you again*

oh, no

the slap in the face
isn't what hurt
the most

it was just a mere
representation
of the metaphorical
slap in the face
that i felt

-   *i did everything for you*

refusing to listen to what a parent says

does not make it okay for them to hit you

defending yourself and standing up to a parent

does not make it okay for them to hit you

telling a parent that they're wrong

does not make it okay for them to hit you

getting angry at a parent

does not make it okay for them to hit you

holding a parent responsible for what they've done

does not make it okay for them to hit you

No child can ever
do anything
that makes it okay
for their parent
to backhand them
across the face
so hard it makes
their entire body numb

& i spent that summer
with
lawyers
judges
cps caseworkers
and cops

                              begging them to
                            protect me from the
                                    one person
                              whose only job
                                was to do so
                                    himself

The people who said
I know you were abused,
I was there
when I escaped my father

Are the same people who said
You were never abused,
I was there
when my father took his life

-   *so, which one is it?*

my goal is to raise children one day
who don't have to recover
from their childhood
the way i had to recover from mine

asking an abuse victim why
they didn't say something sooner
is like asking a caterpillar why
it can not morph into a butterfly sooner

it takes time to grow your wings and
come out of the cocoon you've built for yourself
it takes time to see that you are not a helpless caterpillar
but you are a beautiful butterfly

it takes time to understand that
you do not have to cocoon yourself
in the walls of a home that feels like a living hell
it takes time to realize that you have grown wings
that will allow you to fly so far away from it all

it takes time to realize that
the ~~caterpillar~~ victim is what you were
the ~~butterfly~~ survivor is what you are
that you own everything that happened to you
that you own those wings that you grew
to fly away from the abuse

so don't let them question why
you were in that cocoon for so long
don't let them question where you came from
and don't let them question the process
that had to take place for you to be able to fly away

because they don't understand
what it's like to have to let
metamorphosis take place

-   *the butterfly effect*

writing is my form of escape
it is my coping mechanism
it is the medicine that has
cured me of the illness that trauma is
it has brought peace to my soul
and fullness to my heart

so, don't criticize me for
bringing the darkness into the light
don't hate me for writing about
my abusive parents
and their toxic family members
i didn't turn to drugs and alcohol
like my father did
i didn't turn to religious delusion
like my mother did

writing is the only way for me to heal
as it is the only way for
me to heal others

my words are bodies of water
deep enough to save the souls
of those who need to hear them
powerful enough to drown the souls
of those who refuse to believe them

i will keep those who
can relate to my story
close to my heart
but i will keep those who
hate me for telling my story
on a tight leash

-   *keep your enemies closer.*

Someday
we'll live in a
world where
people tell
domestic violence victims
I believe you
rather than
If it were true, why didn't you
say something sooner?

If you were really abused,
why didn't you
say something sooner?
they ask

I don't know,
maybe it's because
he threatened to
burn the house down
if we told anyone

But, if it's true,
why didn't you ever
call us and say something?
they ask

I don't know,
maybe it's because
he threatened to
cut our hands off
if we called anyone

Mental illness
is the
Cancer
of our Family

Except,
I've never heard
anyone
get blamed for
having
Cancer

the way that
I've heard people
get blamed
for having

depression &

anxiety &

bipolar disorder &

obsessive compulsive disorder &

schizophrenia

- *It's no different*

People would ask me
why I don't live
with my mother

They would ask me
if she were a drug addict
or if she were dead

But how do you explain
to people that
your mother
believes that God
told her to quit her job
and walk away
from her kids?

- *Schizophrenia*

The day that I
~~walked away from~~
escaped from
my father's home
I was told by some that
I was just a spoiled brat
who just wanted to
go away to College

They told me that
my father was a
great father and
we always had food
in our mouths and
clothes on our backs

Although it enraged me
to my deepest core
I didn't bother arguing
with stupidity
because
I knew the truth
about my own life

You had food in your mouths.
When we did have food, it was because we were on food stamps. Other than that – our refrigerator was empty.

You had clothes on your backs.
Ah, yes. The clothes that I paid for – myself.

You had a roof over your head.
Our rent wasn't paid for months.
We were getting evicted, for the third time in a row.

At least you had someplace to keep you warm.
Our heat was shut off.
We had to boil water on the stove just to bathe ourselves.

Your father did everything for his kids.
He could barely drive his kids anywhere because he was always under the influence, let alone do everything for us.

Your father gave you guys everything.
That's why our cell phones were disconnected for over a year, right?

No matter what you say, your father was a hard worker.
Oh, okay. That's why he would lie in bed until noon, and never wake us up for school, right? Not to mention, the fact that I was paying all of his bills – at eighteen-years-old.

You were never abused, you just wanted to go away to college.
Maybe I was so eager to go away to college, to escape the hell I was living in. Did that ever dawn on you?

Well, at least your father loved you.
He did, but – he sure as hell had a funny way of showing it.

if only they were my shadow
they would have seen the times
when i had to boil water
on the stove and carry the pots
to the bathroom one by one
just to bathe myself in hot water

they would have seen the times
when i had to pack all of my belongings
in 48 hours
because there was another eviction

they would have seen the times
when i would open
the refrigerator to nothing but
a gallon of week old milk
and a few bottles of salad dressing

if only they were my shadow
if only they were right behind me
at those moments

maybe they would see through
my constant laughter
and ear to ear smile

maybe they would see that
the light i carry
shines so bright
that it blinds them
from the truth

because it has already seen
the darkest days

Biologically
I am the product
of my parent's dysfunction
mentally I am not

~~daddy issues~~
~~mommy issues~~

-   *what do they call it when you have issues from both?*

they'll warn you about
the monsters under your bed
but what about the ones
you call mom and dad?

Biology doesn't
determine if you are a ~~good~~ parent

A piece of paper
declaring legal guardianship
doesn't either

It's only pure love and
unconditional loyalty
that does

My aunt
shouldn't have to
raise her sister's kids
yet she has been
more of a mother to us
than her sister ever has

- *I thank God for her every day*

my youngest brother
never knew our parents
to live together under the same roof
all he knew his entire life
was divorce & dysfunction
he is also one of the most intelligent
human beings i know

and so she took all of the
pain they caused her and
she turned it into something
b e a u t i f u l

I was told by my father's family
not to show up to his funeral and not to
come around them
ever again.

I was then shamed by my father's family
for not showing up to his funeral and not
wanting to be around them
ever again.

- *damned if you do, damned if you don't*

No wonder why
my father chose to
put such *toxic drugs*
into his body

All he knew
his entire life
were *toxic people*

you are far more precious
than the abuse
you have endured

siblings
aren't
suppose
to be
separated

Please don't
tell me
we weren't
abused
when
your older brother
had a
knife
swung in
his face
by his own
Father

Please don't
tell me
we weren't
abused
when
your younger brother
was told to
stop being
a ~~fucking pussy~~
as he cried in fear
after being
cursed out
by his own
Father

"I thought you knew,"
my sister told me

"How would I have known," I cried

She then confessed,
"I went to dad's apartment the weekend
I said I was sleeping at my friend's house.
It doesn't matter now that he's gone."

\-   *an order of protection wasn't enough*

She
cried
about
the
life
we
had
and
when
we
finally
escaped
it,
she
craved
the
abuse
again

- *it was all she knew*

I'll never
understand
why you
made up
so many lies
and
pretended like
the life
we lived
didn't exist

- *but I forgive you*

Sister –

what kills me the most
is that
you don't understand
how beautiful
how worth it
how amazing
you truly are
please don't let
what our parents
did to us
stop you from
living
your best life

-   *I love you*

Isn't it funny how
you're terrified
of change
yet you
change so
many things
about
yourself?

- *you were beautiful long before the hair-dye & nose piercing*

Do you really think I *wanted*
to sit in court for hours,
fighting a battle against my own Dad?

Do you really think I *wanted*
to get a police escort,
just to get into my home to pack my belongings?

Do you really think I *planned*
to move into my aunt and uncle's home,
to share a bedroom with a nine-year-old?

Do you really think I *planned*
for my entire life to change in just one day?

      -   *questions for the people who said I was selfish*

You're

~~sick in the head~~

~~a spoiled brat~~

~~a cunt~~

~~selfish~~

~~pathetic~~

not the things they say about you

a real father
does not try
to give his
fifteen-year-old son
steroids
disguised
in a
vitamin
bottle

- *manipulation is abuse*

i used to believe that
addiction was a choice, not a disease

i have since learned
that i was wrong

\-   *addiction is a disease, not a choice*

Loving the person
who abused you
doesn't invalidate the abuse
they've put you through

Missing the person
who abused you
doesn't invalidate the abuse
they've put you through

Forgiving the person
who abused you
doesn't invalidate the abuse
they've put you through

It is okay to
love, miss, or forgive
your abuser
but it does not make
what they've
done to you
okay

They said that
my father
was an addict
They said that
they wanted
nothing to do
with him
then, he died

-   *and you were all his best friend, right?*

chapter three
overdose...

the medical examiner
at the hospital
said that
my father died
on
October 3rd 2017
at 10:25pm

                              if only she knew
                         that it wasn't the truth
                                       because
                       the father i once knew
                                           died
                                        a long
                                          time
                                           ago

Mourning a parent
who abused you
isn't a normal
thing
You're constantly
torn between
the heartbreak of
their death
and
the liberation
their death
gave you

My father's last words
to me were that
he was *proud of me*

So, when people
ask me if
I feel any guilt
about his death
I say, *no*

Contrary to what
many think,
it is not
~~my fault~~
anyone's fault
that he
couldn't live
with
~~his own guilt~~
his demons
anymore

"Tell Jacquelyn...
I'm so proud of her
for standing up for you guys
I wish her nothing but the best
and happiness in life
If she can take on me,
she can take on anyone
I didn't realize how well I raised her
And with everything life has to offer
She came out a beautiful, strong young woman
And I'm so proud of her
Tell her... don't let anything stop her
from her dreams and goals"

-   *my father's last words to me, via text message*

I had a dream
that you asked God for
the death penalty
What a relief after
being told it was all
because of me

although we've had our differences
and we went our separate ways,
a piece of me has gone with you

- *rest in peace, dad*

I don't care what

your death certificate says

the drugs

the depression

&

the demons

killed you

long before

you did

losing both an uncle and a father
to drugs in the span of a year
makes you look at the world differently

cocaine was the only thing they had in common
but maybe i was too innocent or too naive at the time
to believe they were only hanging out together
because they both liked to get high

until that night *on september 9th*
i was in the bathtub and my youngest brother
knocked on the door repeatedly
ugh! what do you want? i whined
come downstairs. it's important! he said

i thought it would be another one of our father's talks
about how our mother was doing nothing for us
and how he was going to take her to court
but, little did i know, it was because her brother
o v e r d o s e d
i'm so sorry, guys, your uncle is dead
our father told us
numb was the only thing i felt that night

a few days later
my father showed up to my uncle's funeral
with lines of coke up his nose and
a water bottle filled with cheap vodka in his hands

you'd think that this would've woken him up
but all it did was close his eyes longer
to the damage he was doing

one year and twenty-four days later
the depression, the drugs, and the demons
had killed them both

were you ever abused
says the nurse to my sister
yes
my sister replies

what kind of abuse – physical? verbal? emotional? sexual?
asks the nurse
verbal and emotional

by who
the nurse asks
by my dad

\-   *suicide watch pt. 2*

the last time
i saw my father
was in family court
in front of a judge

he wanted me
to drop the
order of protection
i had against him

a week or two later
he took his life

and i was expected to
act like
that piece of paper
was nothing more
than a piece of paper

i have to give credit
where credit is due
there was a time in
my life where
i loved everything about you
i was a daddy's girl
and you were my whole world
but after i turned sixteen
your bad habits took over your life
you just weren't the father
that i once knew
after the alcohol and drugs
t o o k   o v e r   y o u

but how will we tell our
future sons and daughters
that their grandfather took his life
when he was just forty?

how will we tell them
that he just couldn't get sober
in time to get to meet them
one day?

\-   *a bridge we'll have to cross when we get to it*

Dad –

I'm sorry that I didn't make it to your funeral.

I'm sorry that the people who cared for you the most
(~~your children~~, 3 of your children), weren't there.

I'm sorry that the people who never cared for you
(you know who I'm talking about), were there.

I'm sorry that your family used your death as a way to seek
attention for themselves.

I'm sorry that the only time they posted any appreciation for you
on social media happened when you were no longer alive.

I'm sorry that they did nothing but shame you when you were alive
and nothing but praise you after you died.

It's funny how nobody cares until you take your own life.

- *things I'll never get to say to you*

I was in the fifth grade
when a classmate of mine
picked up a book about
Suicide in the library

She said to me,
"I like suicide better than homicide."

I asked her, *"Why?"*

And she answered,
"Well, I wouldn't want anybody to kill me,
so I'd rather kill myself one day.
I don't want anybody to control when I die."

I looked at her in confusion.

Before then,

I had

no idea

what

Suicide

was.

-    *the irony of innocence*

which is worse
an absent parent
who emotionally abuses you
or a present parent
who verbally abuses you

\-   *a question we're all afraid to answer*

which is worse
mourning a father who committed suicide
or a mother who is still alive

\-   *abandonment*

she handed me an envelope
that read
jacquelyn
paul jr.
larissa
&
justin

she told me specifically
that our father
was not invited to the party

then, he died

and she said
that he was always
the life of the party

don't judge me for
decorating the walls
of my body
when it's the only
place i've ever been
able to call home

-    *tattoos*

I never got to say
goodbye to you
But I hope we'll
meet again someday
Heaven only knows
if you forgive me
For walking away

And what haunts me the most
is not ever being able to know
if you changed your mind
at the last second

When my father died
I was expected to rot in my bed
I was expected to drop out of school
I was expected to stop working my two jobs
and give up on life

My friends would say to me
you look like you're doing okay
I'd smile and say
I don't have a choice

- *just because their life ended, doesn't mean yours should*

It is not your fault
that your loved one
took their life

It is not your fault
that you couldn't save them
from their demons

It is not your fault
that they chose to leave this world

It is not your fault
that they thought
they were ending their pain
but all they did
was hand it over to you

- *to everyone who has lost someone they love to suicide*

The real Angels
are the ones
who already know
what hell looks like

They have sat in the
passenger seat
of the devil's car,
they have let him take
control of the
wheel for far too long

They have walked
through the pits of hell
to get to where they are
They have risen out of the darkness

They have Halos in their eyes
and Heavenly waters in their veins

The light they carry will burn
your doubts of a living God

Because the Heaven in their eyes
is proof that they have survived

The Water in their veins
gives them the ability to remain calm
in situations where others would become afraid

When you see an Angel,
there is no doubting the Heaven within her

It is unexplainable, but you just know that
she wouldn't have been able to grow her wings on her own

You cannot
give an Angel hell
and expect her to
give you Heaven

You cannot
reject a living God
your entire life
and on your deathbed,
ask to be
let into Heaven

You cannot doubt
the existence of Heaven
merely because of your
journey through Hell

You must
trust and believe in the plans
that He has made for you

You must
trust and have faith
that what you
went through
was not in vain

For he who rules the World
would not cause you pain unless he knew
it would serve a greater purpose

Prepare your eyes to see
Prepare your ears to hear
Prepare your heart to accept
the plans He has made for you

you don't need to cut anyone off
they told me
you just need healthy boundaries

\-   *forgive but don't forget*

And no matter
how much hate
you have given me

I still do not
hate you

I hope that one day,
you can find
it in your heart
to change

- *but, I won't hold my breath*

My life was a mess
so that I could turn
it into a message

-   *tell your stories*

come to me
my door is always open
it's unlocked &
i've thrown away the key
come to me
my heart is always open
it bleeds for you
the pain you feel
runs through my veins
come to me
tell me your stories so we can
share them with the world

And that night, the devil came to me
He was disguised as your family

Some people
will comfort you
through your grief

Hold onto
those people

Some people
will berate you
through your grief

Let go of
those people

"How do you do it?"
they asked,
*"How do you stay so strong
despite all you've been through?"*

"I never had a choice,"
she replied.

it was never my choice to be a victim
but
it was his choice to victimize me

Carrying a child
for nine months
does not make
you a mother

Giving a child
your last name
does not make
you a father

Anyone
can do
those things
& label
themselves
a parent

But true parenthood
means complete
and utter selflessness
along with an
undying love
for your children

So, please stop putting
your selfish needs
& helpless addictions
before your children
& acting as if
you're a good parent

- *a message to every deadbeat parent in this world*

how many bottles of whiskey do you need to drink
how many lines of coke do you need to put up your nose
how many pills do you need to swallow
how many houses do you need to get evicted from
how many past due bills need to pile up
how many times does cps need to knock on your door
how many times do you need to get arrested
how many days does your refrigerator have to stay empty
how many mistakes do you have to make
before you realize you're a dead beat parent?

how ironic is it that your sister
put a bottle of Jack Daniel's in your casket

so that
you could lie peacefully,
six feet under
next to the thing that drove you there

i mean,
she might as well have
put the rope in there, too

-   *things i'll never understand*

the devil doesn't
come to you and tell you
he's against you

instead,
he disguises himself
with pretty green eyes
and acts like
he's on your side

and suddenly
out of the blue

he turns

his back

on you

- *we thought we could trust you*

you think you're okay
until the emotional abuse
becomes a throbbing pain in your chest
it wakes you up in the middle of the night
and you can't tell what's worse
the throbbing pain in your chest
or the heaviness in your stomach

you're lying down calmly, but your heart races
and you can't catch your breath
your fears, your worries
the memories, the flashbacks
you have a subconscious archive of them all

you bottled each one of them up
and tossed them into the sea
hoping they would drown so deep
into the water and disappear

but the shore began washing them up one by one
so you gather them all and throw them
into a bulletproof safe
you lock it and you throw the key into a pit of fire
until it disintegrates

you wait a few months
and now all those memories
are banging down the walls of that bulletproof safe
they're trying to escape, but they have no way out

so they leave you with
knives in your chest
and a ton of bricks in your stomach

anxiety begins drowning you
the way you tried to drown the memories

you are worth far more than
the bad cards you were dealt in life

you hear on the news that
two parents in California
were arrested because
their thirteen children were found
chained to their beds
malnourished and neglected
allowed just one meal a day
and one shower a year

yet their parent's social media
painted a picture of
one big happy family

and it all hits you
because
people just couldn't understand
how you and your siblings
could've possibly
been abused and neglected

all because your father's
social media
painted a picture of
one big happy family

society needs to start
realizing that
social media is a lie

we truly never know
what goes on
behind the facebook posts
and instagram pictures

-   *sometimes home is the scariest place*

They don't have faith in God
they're bitter towards him
because *if there were a God*
why would children get abused
why would husbands beat their wives
why would women get raped

You see, there's
this little thing
called *Free Will*
that we all seem
to forget about

So let's stop blaming God
for the Evil in this world
and start blaming the abusers
for their own actions because
I know my God

He lives in
the heart of
every abused child
the home of
every domestic violence victim
the bed of
every rape victim

He is the reason for
their survival,
not the reason for
their trauma

Trust me when I say
He is the reason that
they will be okay

if you don't understand
the liberation
an abuse victim feels
when their abuser
passes away,
think of how liberated
a prisoner must feel
after he or she
gets out of prison
what you need to understand is
that sometimes
prison comes in human form

contrary to what you believe,
you did not live my life

there's too many
forms of Abuse
and not enough
forms of Love

- *this is what's wrong with the world*

there's too many
abused children
in this world
and not enough room
in my college dorm
to adopt them all

- *this is also what's wrong*

two years ago

y-yo-you gotta get those
kids out of that house
no, but you don't understand
janine, janine
you gotta get those kids out of that house
my brother is doing really bad things
you don't even understand
just call the cops, just call cps
march into that house and get those kids out of there!
they're our nieces and nephews, don't you care about them?
how DARE you not do anything to save them?

one year later

hello? j-jah-NEEN!
HOW dare you? how dare you destroy my brother's family?
how DARE you keep those kids from their father?
how dare YOU — how dare you call the police? and cps?

but, wait, hold on.
didn't you TELL me to do that — exactly one year ago?
you screamed at me for not being able to save them.
and i finally did. shouldn't you be happy?

oh, oh yeah — um, i did. you're right.
i am happy. my brother *was* doing really bad things.

four months later

really, JAH-neen?
ah-ah-are you happy now?
this is what you wanted all along, isn't it?
you wanted him to kill himself, didn't you?
this is all your FAULT.
you. lance. jacquelyn. and paul jr.
YOU ALL did this!

139

they say you were never a victim
they say he never really hit you
but they don't know what it feels like
to be handed those domestic violence victim papers
to accept that it happened to you
to admit that it happened to you
to own that it happened to you
that you were a victim
that you are a survivor
they don't know what it feels like
to be scared to death of being traumatized again
they don't know what it feels like
to flinch every time someone gets too close to you
they don't know what it feels like
trying to stay calm every time you hear someone
angrily raise their voice
and they don't know what it feels like
to be petrified of being alone
your anxieties take over your reality
every time you're in a car and the driver stops short, you gasp
because the thought of being in an accident terrifies you
every time you walk home, you do so with keys in between
your knuckles and pepper spray in your fist
and by routine, you walk faster every time
you see a man on the street
you don't trust any one of them
because the one who was suppose to protect you, hurt you
so why wouldn't they?
every time you hear that someone else has been through
what you've been through, you painfully cry
because you can't fathom the idea of how common it is
you wonder why so many parents abuse their children
you wonder why it can't be prevented
you even feel guilty for not doing enough to prevent it
and still, they say you were never a victim
they say he never really hit you

140

your friends and co-workers ask you
if you drink
and instead of conforming to what everyone
is accustomed to doing
you answer with a confident *no*
because drinking is what led
your father to his deathbed
and the taste of alcohol on your lips
reminds you of the smell of it on his breath
when he was screaming in your face
before he made your face feel so numb that you
couldn't smell it on his breath any longer
you can't bear to go down the road of addiction
the same way he did
and you used to feel this way about God, too
you used to question his existence
because your mother says she can't be with her kids
because *God told her so*
you pushed a relationship with God so far away
because of this
but then after the most tragic years of your life
you find yourself crying at an altar
you learn that the Bible says
anyone who does not provide for their own household
has denied the faith and is worse than an unbeliever
you realize that God would never keep a mother
away from her children
you leave church that day
with a new outlook
a new sense of peace
and a new hope
when they ask you now if you believe in God
there is no denying it
because you know
there's no way you could've survived those years
on your own

I do not
mean to
speak sour
of anyone

I speak
only of
the mere
truth

If people
wanted me
to speak sweet
words about them

Well, maybe
they shouldn't
have behaved
so sour

And no,
I
won't
apologize
for
hurting
the
feelings
of
people
who
didn't
ever
care
about
hurting
mine

growing up
under the influence
does not mean that
you cannot
find the strength
to rise above it

my heart beats for
all of the kids
who grew up
under the influence

thank you
for reading...

a letter from me to you

dear reader,

i dug into the deepest parts of myself. i ripped my heart open. and i wrote this for you. it is you that gave me the courage to share my story. knowing that my words are able to bring you comfort is what gave me the strength to write this book.

i want you to know that you are so much more than the bad cards you were dealt in life. and trust me, i know what it's like to have to accept those bad cards. some people were dealt one bad card. others, like myself, were dealt two. i know what its like to be abandoned by a parent. and i also know what it's like to live with an alcoholic parent.

i want my readers to become a community of people who were dealt bad cards and people who know of others that were. i want my readers to come together and bring awareness to child abuse, domestic violence, and absent parents. i want to empower my readers to gain the courage and the strength to share their stories.

i want you to know that there is a way out. you may have to accept those bad cards, but you have the power to trade them in for better ones. if you or someone you know is being abused, please know that there is always a way out. please know that there is help.

national child abuse hot line (1-800) 422-4453
national domestic violence hot line (1-800) 799-7233

xoxo, Jacquelyn Lee

about the author

jacquelyn lee is a twenty-two-year-old from new york. she wrote, edited, and published *under the influence* at nineteen-years-old in only three months. she poured her heart into this project and gave it her all. writing a book of poetry was honestly never something that jacquelyn thought she would do. it all just sort of happened. yet, it's the best thing that has ever happened for her. it's helped her heal, learn, and grow in many ways.

since self-publishing this book, a lot has changed for her. she decided to drop out of fashion school to focus on her writing career. she took some time off from college, and did some soul-searching. in doing so, jacquelyn decided to change her career path. she now plans on spending her life helping others affected by abuse, trauma, addiction, and mental illness.

currently, she's attending stony brook university, where she is pursuing a bachelor's degree in psychology with a minor in writing. she aspires to become a mental health counselor in the future, however, she will never stop writing books. overall, both her mission and her passion is to advocate for mental health.

to stay connected with jacquelyn and for updates on her future books, you can find her as *@jacquelyn.lee* on instagram and as *@_jacquelynlee* on twitter.

about the book

under the influence
is for every child of
an alcoholic parent.

it is for every child of
an addict parent.

it is for every child of
an absent parent.

it is for every child of
an abusive parent.

under the influence is
addiction,
withdrawal,
and overdose.

it is bringing the darkness
into the light.

it is a journey of
abuse,
trauma,
and grief
through poetry.

a letter to my father

i've mourned you in silence. because talking about what happened to you isn't easy. accepting it isn't much easier, either. it's been months. and i still cannot comprehend that you aren't walking on this earth anymore. not a day goes by that i don't think of you. i've cried. i've screamed. i've made mistakes. and through it all, now i can only bring myself to smile. because you are free of your pain. your addiction isn't ruling over your mind anymore. you knew that i was strong enough. you knew that i'd turn what happened to you into a message for the world. and i promise that i will do just that. i promise that i will make you and everyone else proud.

although the bad times outnumbered the good, i will never take the good times we had for granted. although you dragged me down, i will remember the times that you built me up. i will be an example to every child who was brought up in a broken home. the ones who feel guilty for their parent's mistakes. the ones who are confused between heartbreak and liberation when their [abusive] parent passes away. the ones who feel as though their life must end, simply because their parent's did.

your journey in this world may have ended, but mine has just begun. i will hold you in my heart forever — and i will trust and know that everything you've put me through was not for nothing. i know that you are in a better place, in your purest form, with a grateful heart knowing that you left behind a daughter who has broken through the glass ceiling. knowing that you are free has freed me — rest easy, Dad.

Until we meet again...

Jacquelyn

Made in the USA
Monee, IL
21 December 2020

55068738R00085